PRAYING THE SECULAR FRANCISCAN RULE

APPLYING *LECTIO DIVINA* as taught by SAINT BONAVENTURE, O.F.M.

by
Luke Amato

Title:	***PRAYING THE SECULAR FRANCISCAN RULE***
Subtitle:	Applying *Lectio Divina* as taught by St. Bonaventure, O.F.M.
Author:	Luke Amato, O.F.S. LukeAmato@yahoo.com
Copyright:	TXu 1 731 479
ISBN:	13: 978-1-387-03428-4
Imprimatur:	Most Rev. Robert N. Lynch, Bishop of St. Petersburg, Florida September 21, 2010
Nihil Obstat:	Monsignor Bumpus Diocesan Censor September 21, 2010

References to:
    Hebrew Bible: Jerusalem Bible
    Christian Bible: Revised Standard Version
    SFO Rule: From Gospel to Life

TABLE OF CONTENTS

PRELIMINARIES:

Imprimatur & Nihil Obstat..................8

Dedicatory Prayer……………………....9

Introduction to *Lectio Divina*…….……...10

Literal and Spiritual Meanings……….....11

How to Get Started……..………….....16

THE RULE OF THE SECULAR FRANCISCANS

Chapter One: Various Relationships

Paragraph 1: First Day of each month:
In Church:
As one of many Spiritual Families..17

Paragraph 2: Second Day of each month:
In 6Franciscan Family:
Holding a Special Place………......20

Paragraph 3: Third Day of each month:
With 4 Supreme Pontiffs approving
New Expressions of the Rule……...22

Chapter Two: Our Way of Life

a. Our Goals and Predispositions:

    Paragraph 4: Fourth Day of each month observe Gospel of Jesus in Footsteps of St. Francis……..24

    Paragraph 5: Fifth Day of each month Encounter the Person of Jesus………...............................26

    Paragraph 6: Sixth Day of each month Build Up the Church……..…...28

    Paragraph 7: Seventh Day of each month Constant Interior Conversion..31

    Paragraph 8: Eighth Day of each month Prayer & Contemplation..…….33

    Paragraph 9: Ninth Day of each month Imitate Mary, Our Protectress………………....35

b. Our Special Lifestyles as Individuals:

    Paragraph 10: Tenth Day of each month Fulfill Duties of our State of Life……………………………….37

    Paragraph 11: Eleventh Day of each month As Pilgrims, Foster A Spirit of Detachment……..39

Paragraph 12: Twelfth Day of each month
    Purity of Heart frees us to
    Love God & Neighbor..........42

Paragraph 13: Thirteen Day of each month
    Accept all People as
    God's Gift and Image…...……44

Paragraph 14: Fourteenth Day of month
    Do Christian Service to
    Build a Better World……......46

c. <u>Our Group Apostolates and Ministries:</u>

Paragraph 15: Fifteenth Day of each month
    Promote Justice
    Individually and collectively..48

Paragraph 16: Sixteenth Day of each month
    Esteem Work as a Gift &
    Sharing in God's work........50

Paragraph 17: Seventeenth Day of month
    Cultivate Respect for
    Life in the Family………...….51

Paragraph 18: Eighteenth Day of month
    Respect all Creatures in
    Universal Kinship………....…53

Paragraph 19: Nineteenth Day of month
    As Peace Bearers seek
    Unity & Joy, even in Death...55

Chapter Three: Life in Fraternity:

Paragraph 20: Twentieth Day of Month
Levels: Local through
International……………….......58

Paragraph 21: Twenty-first Day of Month
Minister and Council
elected by the Professed…...........60

Paragraph 22: Twenty-second Day of Month
Local Fraternity is the
Basic Unit of the Order………….62

Paragraph 23: Twenty-third Day of the Month
Council Duties & Problems,
Permanent Profession, &
TAU as sign...................................64

Paragraph 24: Twenty-fourth Day of Month
Meetings on all levels
Foster Community……………...66

Paragraph 25: Twenty-fifth Day of the Month
Support Fraternity Needs for
Worship, Ministry, & Charity…68

Paragraph 26: Twenty-Sixth Day of Month
Seek Spiritual Assistance &
Pastoral/Fraternal Visits....………71

ADDITIONAL READINGS FOR EXTRA DAYS OF A MONTH:

27th Day of a Month:
St. Francis: Testament Blessing……….72

28th Day of a Month:
    Exhortation to Brothers & Sisters
    of Penance:
    "Oh, how happy…."……………………...75

29th Day of a Month: His Exhortation
    "They are spouses, brothers
    & mothers…."…………………………..76

30th Day of a Month:
    His Exhortation
    "Oh, how glorious…a…
    Father…Spouse…Brother…."………..78

31st Day of a Month:
    Pope Paul VI's Approval of
        4th Expression of our Rule
            in 800 Years…………………..…80

APPENDIX:

    Other Sources…...………………………………83

        Reinhold Niebuhr's "Serenity Prayer"………..86

        St. Francis of Assisi Peace Prayer…………….88

    Sample Form for *Lectio Divina*………………....90

    List of CD and 6 Books by Author…………….92

IMPRIMATUR

BY

**MOST REVEREND
ROBERT N. LYNCH, BISHOP
ST. PETERSBURG, FLORIDA**

AND

NIHIL OBSTAT

BY

MONSIGNOR BUMPUS,
Diocesan Censor

**We
Sisters and Brothers
of
PENANCE
plead:**

"LORD,

TEACH

US

TO

PRAY."

<u>Introduction</u>

It is recommended that the Professed, Candidates, Inquirers, Associates and Friends of St. Francis are to prayerfully read a section from Holy Scripture daily, especially from the Gospels, applying the *Lectio Divina* method of prayer.

In addition, beginning on the first day of each month, we should resume the prayerful reading of our Holy Rule, starting with paragraph one, along with its accompanying prayer or preferably an extemporaneous prayer from your heart.

By taking the paragraphs in order each succeeding day of the month, we will <u>pray each of the 26 short paragraphs of our Rule before the end of each month.</u>

This will leave the <u>27th through possibly the 31st to consider</u> portions of <u>writings by St. Francis and St. Clare of Assisi,</u> or other related Franciscan writings.

LECTIO DIVINA:
A TIME-PROVEN WAY
TO PRAY SCRIPTURE AND OUR RULE

This effective method of prayer dates back to the earliest days of Christianity, as extolled and practiced by the Fathers of the Church. St. John Cassian, Origen, St Augustine and St. Benedict were but four of the countless great proponents of this approach to prayer.

Our own Pope Emeritus, Benedict XVI, in the Synod Constitution, *Verbum Dei,* strongly urged us to return to this ancient form of prayer. As Franciscans committed to observing the Gospel of Our Lord Jesus Christ, must we not heed the call of the Vicars of Christ as well as that of the Fathers of the Church?

The four steps may be described very briefly as follows:

1. Read (Lectio) slowly a passage from Scripture, no matter how short, until you come to words, phrases or sections that strike a chord in you; jot them down.

2. Reflect (Reflectio) on those sections, words or phrases and consider what they say to you in your personal life. What does it mean to you where you're at?

3.Respond (Oratio) to God in prayer from your heart; just talk to God about it;

4.Receive/Resolve **(Contemplatio/Resolutio)** gratefully whatever spiritual gifts the Lord may choose to give you. That gift may well lead you to make a specific resolution or resolve to improve in that area of our Holy Rule.

Our own <u>Seraphic Doctor, Saint Bonaventure, O.F.M.</u>, has highly developed this approach in his mystical work, *The Tree of Life*. He says: when you reflect and respond to your scripture passage, consider the different meanings in which it can be interpreted.

<u>First</u> and foremost, reflect on <u>the literal sense</u> of scripture, i.e. the obvious meaning of the facts or incident related. But don't stop there! <u>Then proceed to</u> consider <u>the three possible spiritual meanings</u> of the passage.

1. <u>Moral</u>: what is the passage asking me to do or how should I act?

2. <u>Faith</u>: what is this section telling me to trust or who to believe?

3. <u>Eternal</u>: how does this relate to my destiny in the after life?

This faithful son of St. Francis goes deeper in his *Triple Way* and *Itinerarium*, by linking the above three Spiritual meanings to our mystical journey to perfection:

> 1. Purgative Way (Moral): our turning from our sins to God in conversion;
>
> 2. Illuminative Way (Faith): enlightened by our loving imitation of Christ;
>
> 3. Unitive Way (Eternal): union with God, which He perfects for us in eternity.

A detailed example would help immensely here. Let's take one we all know, the *Parable of the Prodigal Son*, which may also be described as the Parable of the *Two Sons* and also The *Merciful Father*:

> A. The Literal Sense is quite obvious to us: the younger son squanders his father's inheritance by sin, suffers want, then returns home to a forgiving father and an envious brother. This sense alone would provide a wealth of material for prayer.
>
> B. The Three Spiritual Senses, however, uncover deeper spiritual treasures for our further meditative prayer:

1. <u>Moral Sense</u>: consider the depravity of our sins:
   a. Younger Son: pigs, mud, starvation
   b. Older Son: the ugliness of envy, sadness over the other's forgiveness

2. <u>Faith</u>: consider this as the story of God's relation to:
   a. Humanity in General:
      i. the younger son - the gentiles or pagans;
      ii. the older son - the Jewish People.
   b. Me in particular: My relation to God is, one time or the other, like that of both sons.

3. <u>Eternity</u>: my future home is in the mansion of my merciful Father in heaven. All of us have an inborn longing to go there.

Notice how well the above three spiritual meanings of the parable fit with St. Bonaventure's mystical theology about the three steps in our spiritual journey to God:

1. **The Purgative** Way is aligned with the Moral Sense;
2. **The Illuminative** Way relates to our faith journey;
3. The **Unitive** Way matches our perfected eternal life with God in heaven.

Nota Bene: At the real risk of over simplification, this writer has deliberately avoided the use of theological language. However, be aware that St Bonaventure does employ the following **technical terms** to name the three spiritual meanings of Scripture:

1. **Topological** for Moral;

2. **Allegorical** for Faith;

3. **Anagogical** or Eschatology for Eternal Life.

Now, that's more than enough of the theory. Your head should be swimming by now! Actually as you practice this method of prayer, you'll find it simple but rewarding. So, please turn the page of this stage of your life and let's get down to the practical steps and start.

HOW TO START:

A. <u>First pick a suitable time and place,</u> for example:

    1. Early morning on the porch,
    2. Lunch break on the park bench,
    3. Late at night in your favorite easy chair.

B. <u>Choose a paragraph from our Rule.</u>

C. <u>Let the awareness that you're in God's presence calmly sink in and remain with you throughout.</u>

D. <u>Then start to pray using the *Lectio Divina* approach:</u>

    1. Read (and re-read) slowly
    2. Reflect
    3. Respond
    4. Receive (Resolve)*

*When you're done, don't forget to thank God for whatever He's given you in this prayer, even if you're not aware of His gifts. He blesses us for just trying. One of His best gifts may be your firm decision to make a definite resolution or resolve to improve in that very specific area of our Holy Rule.

RULE OF THE SECULAR FRANCISCAN ORDER

CHAPTER I:

PARAGRAPHS 1 TO 3: THE PLACE OF THE SECULAR FRANCISCAN ORDER

PARAGRAPH 1: First Day of the Month

Read:

The Franciscan family as <u>one among *many spiritual families raised up by the Holy Spirit*</u> in the church, <u>unites all members</u> of the people of God – laity, religious, and priests – who recognize that they are called to <u>follow Christ in the footsteps of Saint Francis</u> of Assisi. In various ways and forms but in <u>life-giving union</u> with each other, they intend to <u>make present the charism</u> of their common Seraphic Father in the life and mission of the Church.

Reflect:

As baptized Catholics, all of us are called

to lives of holiness. The Church provides all the means and guidance to reach the heights of sanctity, especially through the sacraments. From its very foundation, God has raised up holy men and women inspired to follow Jesus in unique ways. Often they attracted others to seek holiness along with them and the Church put its stamp of approval on their ways of living the Gospel life. We as Franciscans are an example of one of those spiritual families. I can picture Francis joyfully repairing churches. Passersby were attracted to his sense of joy and joined, first as friars, others as poor ladies, and finally as women and men living in the world: thus our Three Orders. As each of our three orders seek to be faithful to our specific callings, we also give and take from each other's spiritual experiences as Franciscans. As such we are all to uniquely contribute to the work of Holy Mother Church.

Respond:

O Holy Spirit, thank you for raising up so many varied and beautiful spiritual families in Your Church. Along with the Franciscan Order, I lift them all up to You in prayer, be they Augustinian, Benedictine, Carmelite, or Dominican and all others. These spiritual families are all proven paths leading to a closer imitation of You, O Christ. Father, may You attract countless worthy candidates to them and to us, as priests, religious and laity. I beg the intercession of their inspired saints: Francis and Clare of Assisi, Augustine and his mother Monica, Benedict and his sister Scholastica, Theresa and John of the Cross, Catherine and our spiritual cousin, Dominic, and all the other spiritual leaders.

Receive (Resolve):

Ephesians 3:15 *"For this reason I bow my knees before the Father, from whom every family in heaven and on earth is named...."*

PARAGRAPH 2: Second Day of the Month

Read:

The <u>Secular Franciscan Order holds a special place in this family circle</u>. It is an organic union of <u>all Catholic fraternities</u> scattered throughout the world and <u>open to every group</u> of the faithful. In these fraternities the brothers and sisters, led by the Spirit, <u>strive for perfect charity in their own secular state</u>. By their profession they pledge themselves to live the gospel in the manner of Saint Francis by means of <u>this rule</u> approved by the Church.

Reflect:

As a real order of seculars, we are privileged to belong to this great spiritual family. The First and Second Orders share with us their teaching, prayers and example. We on our part try to put the Franciscan charism into practice in the workaday world and reciprocate by giving feedback to the first two orders. We too are called to perfect charity in our own state. And it never ceases to amaze me that we are a real order and are spread all over the world. Even Christians of other traditions have been attracted to Christ through Francis' way of life: this can become a bridge leading them back to

the Church. The Episcopal Friars of Atonement Friars in N.Y.S. are a powerful example of that.

Respond:

Lord, thank you for inspiring St. Francis to invite us into this Franciscan Family. As seculars, show us how we can "be in the world, but not of the world". What is this unique role that you have given us as seculars? You've united us in fraternal bonds with Catholic brothers and sisters of every race, sex and age in every land. We also place before you those of other Christian traditions that share our regard for St. Francis and his ideals. Jesus, grant us that unity for which you prayed, so that there will one Shepherd and one flock. Guide us in our unique relationship with the rest of the Franciscan Family of priests, sisters and brothers. Help us to truly share our special charism with one another, open to both giving and receiving, according to our circumstances and expertise.

Receive (Resolve):

Deuteronomy 7:6 *"The Lord your God has chosen you out of all the peoples on the face of the earth to be His people, His treasured possession."*

PARAGRAPH 3: Third Day of the Month

Read:

The present rule (approved by <u>Pope Paul VI</u>), succeeding *"Memoriale Propositi"* (by Pope <u>Innocent III</u> in 1221) and the rules approved by the Supreme Pontiffs <u>Nicholas IV and Leo XIII</u>, adapt the Secular Franciscan Order to the <u>needs and expectations of our Holy Church in the conditions of changing times.</u> Its interpretation belongs to the Holy See and its application will be made by the General Constitutions and particular statutes.

Reflect:

Right from the very outset, St. Francis set the example of faithful relations with the Holy Fathers in Rome. It is to this fidelity that we can credit our longevity and growth within the Church. Other movements before and since have come and gone mainly because they lacked that strong relationship. But our Holy Rule is a living document that is irrevocably tied to our faith in and commitment to the Church, which keeps us relevant to its needs in the spirit of St. Francis.

Respond:

How can we thank You enough, Father, for giving us the guidance of Your Church in understanding and applying our Holy Rule. Over these past 800 years, Your Spirit has moved four popes to adapt it to the needs of the Church and times: we lift up to You Innocent III, Nicholas IV, Leo XIII, and Paul VI. Bless them, Jesus, for as Your Vicars they have led us along Your right path, preserving the spirit of the Rule of St. Francis in our times. Keep us always faithful to all our Holy Fathers and our Profession.

Receive (Resolve):

Matthew 16:19 *"I will give you the keys of the kingdom of heaven, and whatever you bind on earth shall be bound in heaven, and whatever you loose on earth shall be loosed in heaven."*

CHAPTER II: PARAGRAPHS 4 TO 9: INTERIOR PREDISPOSITIONS & AIMS
1
PARAGRAPH 4: Fourth Day of the Month

Read:

The rule and life of the Secular Franciscans is this: to observe the Gospel of our Lord Jesus Christ by following the example of Saint Francis of Assisi, who made Christ the inspiration and the center of his life with God and people. Christ, the gift of the Father's love, is the Way to Him, the Truth into which the Holy Spirit leads us, and the Life which He has come to give abundantly. Secular Franciscans should devote themselves to careful reading of the gospel, going from gospel to life and life to the gospel.

Reflect:

For me this paragraph, along with the one following, represent the heart of our rule: to have a deeply growing personal relationship with Jesus. As a life long Catholic I had been taught much about Jesus, and the way He wants me to live. But I'm sorry to say that all too often He had seemed distant to me, out there somewhere, not real for me. However, over the years my growing attraction to Francis keeps revealing more and more about the reality of Jesus in his life, and also in mine. I imagine that it must have been like that for the people who came in contact with Francis, as his ongoing conversions led him to a more personal relation with Jesus. Like Francis, I keep seeing myself in those two disciples on the road to Emmaus. Previously they had been viewing him merely as a great prophet; but the crucifixion took even that meager faith from them. However, when Jesus did set their hearts burning by opening scripture for them, they were prepared to recognize Him personally in the breaking of the bread. That's also the way Francis got to know Jesus: through scripture and Holy Communion with Him. That has to be my way, too.

Respond:

This is our way of life: to follow You, Jesus, as You reveal Yourself in the Holy Gospel, just as you opened Scriptures to St. Francis. Stir up the Holy Spirit which You have given us by our Baptism and Confirmation, so that we may hear what You are telling us today. You inspired Your servant Francis to bring his life situations to the Gospel and You showed how You wanted him to serve You. And as he prayed Your Word daily, You enlightened his path. With him, I too must exclaim: *"That's what I want!"*

Set my heart burning within me, as You did with the two disciples on the road to Emmaus, when You opened up Scripture for them. Jesus, help me love You more and more.

Receive (Resolve):

Colossians 1:15-18 *"He is the image of the invisible God, the first-born of all creation, for in Him all things were created, in heaven and on earth...."*

PARAGRAPH 5: Fifth Day of the Month

Read:

Secular Franciscans, therefore, should seek to encounter the living and active person of Christ in their brothers and sisters, in Sacred Scripture, in the Church and in liturgical activity. The faith of Saint Francis, who often said, *"I see nothing bodily of the Most High Son of God in this world except His Most Holy Body and Blood,"* **should be the inspiration and pattern of their Eucharistic life.**

Reflect:

Here the rule clearly emphasizes our aim: "to encounter the living and active person of

Christ". That's not just a pious thought! Our Jesus is a real person; though he died once for sin, resurrected He now lives forever and is personally working in my life through the Sacred Mysteries. This is how He exercises His Lordship in my life right now. And this rule shows me explicitly how I am to make personal contact with Him. The epitome of my contact with Him has to be in my daily reception of Holy Communion; in those precious moments above all others, I'm in His special presence. By faith I know that He's really there with me; I can personally "see by faith" my Most High Lord, even though my senses perceive what appears to be "bread" and "wine". But, alas, those moments of real communion are fleeting. What about those hours in between this morning and tomorrow? There is always the beautiful practice of Spiritual Communion with my Lord! In fact, any prayerful communication with Him places me in His presence and such opportunities abound throughout the day: be it in the Church's liturgy or by interaction with other people.

Respond:

Father, I want to know Jesus in a deeper, more personal way. I need Him to be Lord in my life. As You know, I don't make out so well when I take control of my own affairs. Jesus, from the bottom of my heart, I ask you to become ever more real to me. Alone I can do nothing, but I can do all things in You who strengthen me. Holy Spirit, rouse Your power within me and show me the countless opportunities to encounter Jesus often in my daily life. I especially look forward to those precious few moments when I receive You daily in Holy Communion. But there are many other chances to meet with You in my brothers and sisters.

Receive (Resolve):

Rev 22:20 *"Come, Lord Jesus."*

PARAGRAPH 6: Sixth Day of the Month

Read:

They have been made living members of the Church by being buried and raised with Christ in baptism; they have been united more intimately with the Church by profession. Therefore, they should go forth as witnesses and instruments of her mission among all people, proclaiming Christ by their life and words. Called like Saint Francis to rebuild the Church and inspired by his example, let them devote themselves energetically to living in full communion with the pope, bishops, and priests, fostering an open and trusting dialogue of apostolic effectiveness and creativity.

Reflect

I cannot separate my personal relationship with Jesus from my relationship to His Body, the Church; it's just as real. That relationship began for me by my baptism, deepened by my reception of confirmation, and later flowered in my profession of the Rule. But that relationship with the Church has far reaching effects for the rest of my life as a Franciscan. "Rebuild My Church...." Sure he took that command so literally, and thank God he did. Wasn't that what attracted followers, leading him to seek approval of the Holy Father? So right from the outset, Francis placed himself and us his followers squarely under the protection and guidance of Holy Mother Church. And as long as we are faithful to that relationship, God will *prosper the works of our hands*.

Respond:

"Go rebuild My house, which you can see is falling down." This was the command you inspired in St. Francis before the Crucifix at the Chapel of San Damiano. He took Your words

literally, O Lord, and set about manually repairing the Church building. But You had a deeper meaning for him and for us: You thus attracted others to follow him, resulting in the formation of a new family made up of Three Orders. In order to build up Your Body, the Church, Jesus, sometimes I have to take Your words at face value, even when it means doing what others might consider menial tasks for Your Church. Then You can show me, in Your own sweet time, how You really want me to serve. But I know this already: my service must be done in loyalty to You and Your Vicar on earth, along with Your bishops, priests, and deacons, be they secular or religious. You know better than I how damaged Your Church has been by these accusations of sex scandals, whether fairly or unfairly leveled. Show me how I can help build up Your Body.

Receive (Resolve):

"...like living stones be yourselves built into a spiritual house.... ."

PARAGRAPH 7: Seventh Day of the Month

Read:

United by their vocation as *"brothers and sisters of penance,"* and motivated by the dynamic power of the gospel, let them conform their thoughts and deeds to those of Christ by means of that radical interior change which the gospel itself calls conversion. Human frailty makes it necessary that this conversion be carried out daily. On this road to renewal, the Sacrament of Reconciliation is the privileged sign of the Father's mercy and the source of grace.

Reflect:

Repent! The prophets called for it. John the Baptist repeated it. And Jesus Himself reinforced the message. Is it any wonder that Francis would pick up the same invitation to conversion? In his Exhortation to us, didn't he call us Secular Franciscans, his *Brothers and Sisters of Penance*? If I am to truly follow Jesus like Francis did, I must have the mind of Jesus within me, to become ever more like Jesus. That means that I have to change my ways so they conform to those of our Lord. That has to be a daily process. When I detect within myself attitudes and actions that are not Christ-like, they must be rooted out. Considering my fallen nature, I'm going to need the daily help of God's grace, first to recognize what needs changing, be truly sorry, and seek His assistance. Thank God for the Sacrament of Reconciliation!

Respond:

As Brothers and Sisters of Penance, O Father, help us not only to turn away from sin in true *metanoia*, but to turn us ever more closely toward union with Your Son. May the Mind of Jesus become our mind…His actions our actions. O Most Holy Spirit, enlighten us so that we may more fruitfully participate in the Sacrament of Reconciliation on a regular basis, at least monthly. But, You O God, know my weaknesses. Therefore, call me to ever deeper conversion every day of my life.

Receive (Resolve):

Acts 3:19 *"Repent therefore, and turn again, that your sins may be blotted out, that times of refreshing may come from the presence of the Lord…."*

PARAGRAPH 8: Eighth Day of the Month

Read:

As Jesus was the true worshiper of the Father, so let prayer and contemplation be the soul of all they are and do. Let them participate in the sacramental life of the Church, above all the Eucharist. Let them join in the liturgical prayer in one of the forms proposed by the Church, reliving the mysteries of the life of Christ.

Reflect:

"...Let prayer and contemplation be the soul of all they are and do...." What a powerful invitation, not just to pray, but rather to become prayer itself. We look to the example of Jesus Himself. Didn't the disciples themselves ask Him to teach them how to pray? Our Lady, too, calls on us to pray the Crown of her Seven Joys, but she tells us it must be prayer from the heart. We learn this also from our Holy Father Francis and our great family of Saints and Blessed. Even our own Saint Bonaventure joins the teachings of the Fathers of the Church on *Lectio Divina* as part of our search. The Church calls us to prayerfully live her sacra-mental life, to join her in the liturgy of the hours. Like the author of *The Way of the Pilgrim,* we want to learn how to fulfill the command to pray

always, so that even our very breath becomes a prayer. But isn't contemplation itself a gift from the Holy Spirit?

Respond:

Lord Jesus, true God and true Man, You constantly turned to Your Father in prayer. If You were so moved, perfect as You are, imagine my need to pray, weak as I am. O how tenderly you spoke to Your Father from Your Heart! Make my heart like unto Thine. Lord, teach me to pray from the heart, even as You taught Your apostles. You have commanded us to call Your Father *"Our Father"*. Let prayer and contemplation become an integral part of everything that I am and do. Jesus, You have given me Your Spirit in Baptism and Confirmation; now I ask You: unleash His power within me to praise Your Holy Name and follow His gentle inspirations. Oh Holy Spirit, draw me more deeply into the prayer life of Your Church. Whether alone or with others in fraternity, help us to experience in our depths Your power in the Sacramental Life of the Church, especially through the presence of Jesus in the Holy Eucharist and in Liturgical Prayer. Never allow our prayers to become rote, but instead deepen our relationship to each Divine Person of the Blessed Trinity: Father, Son and Holy Spirit.

Receive (Resolve):

Romans 8:26 *"....we do not know how to pray as we ought, but the Spirit Himself intercedes for us with sighs too deep for words."*

PARAGRAPH 9: Ninth Day of the Month

Read:

The Virgin Mary, humble servant of the Lord, was open to His every word and call. She was embraced by Francis with indescribable love and declared the protectress and advocate of his family. The Secular Franciscans should express their ardent love for her by imitating her complete self-giving and by praying earnestly and confidently.

Reflect:

I burst with joy when I consider how we as Franciscans are called to honor and imitate Our Lady. Francis himself explains in his Exhortation to us how we can become mothers of our Savior. Oh, how the sons and daughters of St. Francis have risen up during the centuries to explain and defend the prerogatives which God Himself showered on her. We can never give her more honor than the Father gave her.

But the greatest honor I can give her is to imitate her total submission to God and His will. Such devotion to her is the clearest sign of our vocation to the Secular Franciscan Order. She teaches me another lesson: her Seven Sorrows were really only the reverse side of her Seven Joys of our Franciscan Crown. Hasn't that been true so often in my own life?

Respond:

Father, how can we thank you enough for choosing Mary to be the Mother of Your Son. Although a mere human being, she is as the poet says *"our tainted nature's solitary boast."* Thank You for showing Blessed Duns Scotus, O.F.M. how she could have been Immaculately Conceived, and yet still be Redeemed by Jesus, her Savior and ours. You certainly have the *power to do it, and it was fitting that You do it; so You did it!* Yes, Father, she is Your especially chosen daughter, filled with all grace, making her a worthy Mother of Your Son, the Second Person of the Blessed Trinity. By her humble "fiat", she was open to the life giving action of the Holy Spirit as Spouse. Yes, Mary lives a unique relationship with each Person of the Blessed Trinity, yet a relationship that each of us is called to experience, albeit in a different way. In his admonition to us faithful, Our Holy Father Francis explained how I too am called to be a child of the Father, by doing His will like my Older Brother Jesus. I also must be opened to the action of the Holy Spirit within me, so that like Mary, Jesus can live in me by love and then I can give "birth" to Him by good example. Oh Mary, Patroness of the Franciscan Order, pray for me that like you, I may declare my *"fiat"* without reservation.

Receive (Resolve):

Luke 1:46-49 "Mary said: *'My soul magnifies the Lord, and my spirit rejoices in God my Savior, for He has regarded the low estate of His handmaiden. For behold, henceforth all generations will call me blessed; for He who is mighty has done great things for me, and holy is His Name.'"*

PARAGRAPHS 10 TO 14:

HOW SECULAR FRANCISCANS ARE TO LIVE:

PARAGRAPH 10: Tenth Day of the Month

Read:

United themselves to the redemptive obedience of Jesus, who placed His will into the Father's hands, let them faithfully fulfill the duties proper to their various circumstances of life. Let them also follow the poor and crucified Christ, witness to Him even in difficulties and persecutions.

Reflect:

It seems to me that the paragraphs that went before this one in Chapter II were all about the aims and pre-conditions of my call to be a Franciscan. From here on in, I expect to find the *"how to's"* for living this life. And I don't have to look too far. This part of the rule makes it very clear: do what my state in life calls me to do, in whatever situations which the Lord has in store for me. Here I could let my imagination run wild, conjuring up terrible circumstances of sickness, financial hardship, even abandonment. But what's to be gained by doing that? Nothing positive! Better to learn from those recovering from the various compulsions: *take one day at a time.*

Respond:

Lord, I don't have to start looking for any extra penances today, I just have to fulfill the obligations of my state of life: as a spouse and foster parent, as a child to my parents and a sibling to my brothers and sisters, as worker and retiree, as a human being and a Christian.

Each of these circumstances in which You have placed me entail a whole host of duties and sacrifices in order to be performed well in Your sight. But, most of all I need Your grace. Without You I can do nothing, yet I can do all things in You who strengthen me. No, I don't know what sufferings and sicknesses may lie in store for me (and I don't really want to know ahead of time). *Sufficient for today are the troubles thereof.* Father, just help me to unite all my situations to the saving work of Jesus Your Son, Who, led by the Spirit, sought always to do Your will.

Receive (Resolve):

Micah 4:2 *"Come let us go up to the mountain of the Lord, to the house of the God of Jacob. He will teach us His ways so that we may walk in His paths."*

PARAGRAPH 11: Eleventh Day of the Month

Read:

Trusting in the Father, Christ chose for Himself and His Mother a poor and humble life, even though He valued created things attentively and lovingly. Let the Secular Franciscans seek a proper spirit of detachment from temporal goods by simplifying their own material needs. Let them be mindful that according to the gospel they are stewards of the goods received for the benefit of God's children. Thus, in the spirit of "the Beatitudes," and as pilgrims and strangers on their way to the home of the Father, they strive to purify their hearts from every tendency and yearning for possession and power.

Reflect:

I've often wondered why Jesus chose a life of poverty, when He could have come in splendor. Certainly the Israelites were expecting something quite a bit more majestic and pompous. This brings Blessed Duns Scotus, O.F.M., to mind again: if our first parents had not sinned, then He would have come in all His glory, much as He will do at the end of time. Well, man did sin and He did choose to come as a poor suffering Savior. Would we really be so attracted to him if he came any other way? Wasn't this what so appealed to us about Francis' imitation of Christ. This very poverty at one and the same time fascinated, yet frightened, me about the Franciscans. Here I was: a family man, with financial obligations. My state in life would not allow me to embrace a life of strict poverty, like those in the First

Order or Poor Clares. Thank goodness there were tertiaries who by their example showed me how I could be called to be *"poor in spirit"*, striving for a life of true stewardship, using the good things of this world with moderation and detachment. It was for me to find ways to use the things that God gave me for His purposes, without letting things own me.

Respond:

Lord Jesus, I know that as a Secular Franciscan, I cannot strictly follow You and Your Mother in poverty, like the *Poverello* St. Francis did. Work and family obligations may prevent me from doing so; but in its place, please give me that same spirit of detachment which so marked the poor life that You so voluntarily chose for Your Mother and Yourself. You made all creatures good and You could have picked the most comfortable life for Yourself. Teach me, as You taught Your servant Francis how to honor You in Your creatures, and yet at the same time not let them get in the way of my personal relationship with You. Continue helping me to reduce my dependence on "stuff" so that I may be more generous in giving to the poor and the Church. Lord, keep reminding me that everything I have is a gift on loan from You and so I must use it carefully to benefit all in need. Fill me with that

"Poverty of Spirit" about which you preached so eloquently on the Mount; it's the only true path to real happiness on my journey back to You. Help me to so order and simplify my life that my passing will not cause strife over whatever little or much I leave in this world.

Receive (Resolve):

Matthew 6:26, 28, 33 *"Look at the birds of the air...Consider the lilies of the field....seek first His kingdom and His righteousness, and all these things shall be added unto you."*

PARAGRAPH 12: Twelfth Day of the Month

Read:

Witnessing to the good yet to come and obliged to acquire purity of heart because of the vocation they have embraced, they should set themselves free to love God and their brothers and sisters.

Reflect:

Often I feel pulled in two directions. I know the things that I am called to do, yet I find myself doing the opposite. Sure, I know that's the result of my fallen nature. St. Paul speaks clearly to me of that struggle; I, too, experience that double pull in my own life. Now, when I read about "purity of heart" in the Beatitudes, I think Jesus may not only be talking about sexual purity, but perhaps more particularly of purity of intention, a singleness of purpose: *love of God and love of neighbor.* My commitment to poverty is also part of the answer to this inner struggle. Hear, oh man, you are called to love the Lord your God, with your whole heart ... and your neighbor as yourself. Anything that gets in your way of doing that is not from God.

Respond:

Jesus, You promised us that the truth will set us free. You are the way, the truth and the life. Yet my faults often limit my freedom to fully love You and others because of You. I so often lack that confidence in You, that purity of heart, that singleness of purpose, that clarity of vision, that courage of convictions. These hold back my ability to completely give myself in love. In such a state, how can I joyfully bear witness to the good things that You have in store for us? Break these bonds that bind me! Help me really *let go and let You*, God, set me free to love You openly and completely. I can do all things in You who strengthen me.

Receive (Resolve):

Romans 7:23 *"...I see in my members another law at war with the law of my mind...."*

PARAGRAPH 13: Thirteenth Day of the Month

Read:

As the Father sees in every person the features of His Son, the firstborn of many brothers and sisters, so the Secular Franciscans with a gentle and courteous spirit accept all people as a gift of the Lord and an image of Christ. A sense of community will make them joyful and ready to place themselves on an equal basis with all people, especially with the lowly for whom they shall strive to create conditions of life worthy of people redeemed by Christ.

Reflect:

I believe that one of the big reasons why people were (and still are) attracted to Francis is that they feel safe with him. If he related to even inanimate creatures as his brothers and sisters, imagine how he came across to all his fellow human beings. Weren't they created in the image of God's Son and redeemed by His

Precious Blood? That's not always the way I respond to certain groups of people, for example the homeless. Oh, deep down I know they're my brothers, but I'm also aware that I experience an inner revulsion, not too unlike Francis' initial reaction to lepers. Well, if I can't physically embrace them, can't I at least recognize that, *there for the grace of God go I?* More, can't I work to ameliorate their hunger and deprivation?

Respond:

Heavenly Father, You used Jesus as the model for all of Your creation and so all things reflect His image. But it is especially in us humans, with our intellect and free will, that You see Your Son. Should I behold less? Holy Spirit, gently nudge me to accept others as a fragile gift from You. No, even more, help me cherish them in an ever so gentle manner, because through them I encounter Jesus Himself. And even more than that, make me one with them in joyful community no matter what their status or background. All life has dignity in Your eyes, not only by Your creation, but also by redemptive work. You've always had a special love for the poor; so should I. So, remove all vestiges of bias from me.

Receive (Resolve):

Matthew 7:12 *"Do unto others as you would have them do unto you: for this is the Law and the Prophets."*

PARAGRAPH 14: Fourteenth Day of a Month

Read:

Secular Franciscans, together will all people of good will are called to build a more fraternal and evangelical world so that the kingdom of God may be brought about more effectively. Mindful that anyone *"who follows Christ, the perfect man, becomes more of a man himself,"* let them exercise their responsibilities competently in the Christian spirit of service.

Reflect:

Jesus Himself emphasized that He came to serve and not be served, to minister to others and not be ministered to. Am I called to anything less than to work with others to build a kingdom of justice and peace on this earth, in preparation for His kingdom to come? God has blessed me with a good education and certain talents. Shouldn't I use those gifts for the benefit of others? I should use them with all the competence at my disposal. Anything less would be cheating the Good God that gave them to me.

Respond:

Father, You have called me to serve You in a Christian spirit. For this purpose You have placed me in these circumstances: this definite time and place, with certain abilities (limited though they are), along with my own background and experiences. These are the "talents" about which Your Son spoke in His parables. With these talents and Your grace, I am to build a better world in my sphere of influence, a world more in line with Gospel and brotherly values. You taught me to pray daily that *"Thy kingdom come; Thy will be done, on earth as it is in heaven."*

Receive (Resolve):

Matthew 25: 34, 40 *"Come, O blessed of My Father, inherit the kingdom prepared for you from the beginning, from the foundation of the world; for I was hungry and you gave food...As you did it to one of the least of these My brethren, you did it to Me."*

PARAGRAPHS 15 TO 19:

SPECIAL FRANCISCAN APOSTOLATES:

PARAGRAPH 15: Fifteenth Day of the Month

Read:

Let them individually and collectively be in the forefront in promoting justice by the testimony of their human lives and their courageous initiatives. Especially in the field of public life, they should make definite choices in harmony with their faith.

Reflect:

At first I never thought that there were certain apostolates that were considered particularly Franciscan. And in a very real sense, all true ministries are open to us as our service to mankind. But, justice stands out as paramount, for there can never be any real progress unless justice is satisfied first; we must give our fellow man what is his due. And, this we should do, not only working on our own, but also working in cooperation with groups which share our aims. However, I am not to compartmentalize my life as an individual; my work for justice must be reflected equally in my public life.

Respond:

You are All Just, O God. And I would rather trust Your justice than the "mercy" of men. But You call me, by my vocation as a Franciscan, to work for justice on all levels of society, starting first and foremost where I find myself, be it privately at home, or publicly at work or in my community. I must become just and fair not only in my heart and intentions, but also externally in all my actions. What I should be on the inside, I must also become on the outside. You know that this is not very easy to do in this "dog eat dog" society. Sometimes I have to take a loss and assume hardship, if I am to continue to be a man of my word. But I don't necessarily have to "go it alone." I have sisters and brothers in the fraternity who will go with me. And there are others of good will who don't even share our faith. Give me the courage to walk shoulder to shoulder with them, even in the face of ridicule and opposition. And even if none go with me, there's always You. I'll never really be alone in this apostolate for justice.

Receive (Resolve):

Proverbs 21:2-3 *"...the Lord weighs the heart. To do what is right and just is more acceptable to the Lord than sacrifice.*

PARAGRAPH 16: Sixteenth Day of the Month

Read:

Let them esteem work both as a gift and as a sharing in the creation, redemption, and service of the human community.

Reflect:

I have to face the unpleasant fact that all too often in the past, I've looked on my work as a necessary evil: what I had to do just to earn my daily bread. How foreign that attitude was to Francis. He loved work and encouraged all his followers to work. And no task was too menial. Far from a mere duty, he considered it a real privilege. In his Exhortation to us tertiaries, he taught that we are invited into the very life of God who created, redeemed and sanctified us.

Respond:

O Most Blessed Trinity, what a privilege is extended to me to share in the great work of each Divine Person! With You Father, I'm invited to partake of Your ongoing creation. While You, Jesus, allow me, as a member of Your Mystical Body, to be a partner in Your great Redemptive work of salvation. Most Holy Spirit, You even let me join You in Your sanctification role, as *You renew the face of the earth.* Here is my basic apostolate as a layman. Your blessed clergy and religious teach and form me according to Your Will, so that I may go out into the work-a-day world to carry out Your Good News by word and example. O what a doubly blessed gift: I'm blessed when I perform labor and when I receive work. And no labor is too menial, too insignificant: my Lord and Savior sanctified it by the sweat of His own brow. Thank You, O God, for the blessings of work.

Receive (Resolve):

I Thessalonians 1: 23   *"We give thanks... remembering before our God and Father your work of faith and labor of love...."*

PARAGRAPH 17: Seventeenth Day of the Month

Read:

In their family they should cultivate the Franciscan spirit of peace, fidelity, and respect for life, striving to make of it a sign of a world already renewed in Christ. By living the grace of matrimony, husbands and wives in particular should bear witness in the world to the love of Christ for His Church. They should joyfully accompany their children on their human and spiritual journey by providing a simple and open Christian education and being attentive to the vocation of each child.

Reflect:

Especially in the area of family life, we are called to live out our profession. It should permeate all our actions and relationships, even when the whole family may not have committed themselves to our way of life. A very humorous but revealing incident comes to mind. At a discussion during a social gathering of our fraternity and our family members, one preteen boy referred to himself as *"we Franciscans"*. The entire group broke out into laughter and one of us explained that it involved a long process to become a Franciscan. But, as we further reflected on the incident, we rejoiced that he so identified with us. Isn't that how our members should influence all members of our families and associates?

Respond:

Jesus, Mary and Joseph, what a beautiful example of Family Life You have given us, whether we're single, married, or widowed.

Such respect and reverence for life! O how we need that example today more than ever. We see so much disrespect for life: be it divorce and remarriage, neglect and abuse of children, a lack of openness to life, not to speak of the unspeakable acts of abortion and euthanasia. Oh, Holy Father Francis, you personally experienced a difficult family life. You taught us to preach always and when necessary use words. Please intercede for our Franciscan families; all of us fall short of the ideals of the Holy Family. Help us to mirror by our example the Gospel values of a true "Culture of Life."

Receive (Resolve):

Joshua 24:15 *"...choose for yourselves this day whom you will serve....But as for me and my household, we shall serve the Lord."*

PARAGRAPH 18: Eighteenth Day of the Month

Read:

Moreover they should respect all creatures, animate and inanimate, which *"bear the imprint of the Most High,"* and they should strive to move from the temptation of exploiting creation to the Franciscan concept of universal kinship.

Reflect:

"Take St. Francis of Assisi out of the garden!" That was the theme of a talk given by a Franciscan Sister to our fraternity. I was at first taken back by her topic until she explained what she meant. Then the truth of it dawned on me. This is an area where we need Francis and his views on creation, whether in the market place or in our personal lives. More and more our society is beginning to see the harm that we're doing to our earth's air, water, and soil. In Genesis, God made us stewards of His creation to care for it, not to exploit it. Our Lord Himself revealed His care for the birds of the air and the lilies of the field. Francis showed us that there exists a real kinship with all creatures: with the stones we share existence; with the plants life, and with animals feeling. All of us together reflect the beautiful attributes of the very God that made us. Not only should we respect creation, even more so should we revere it as coming from God.

Respond:

"Most High, All Powerful, All Good, Lord….All praise be Yours, my Lord, through all that You have made…." With these words, Holy Father Francis, you show us how all creatures reflect the Glory of God and how we should treat even

inanimate creatures with reverence. You go so far as considering them our brother and sister creatures. With such a kinship, how could we dare misuse them! Lord God, thank you for this timely apostolate, as the world begins to realize more clearly the extent of self-destruction we wreak on our own environment. As his heirs, show the world the fuller meaning of the statues of *"Saint Francis in the Garden"* and take him well beyond there. Let me take him into all creature relationships, especially those human conflicts that need the healing hand of forgiveness.

Receive (Resolve): Psalm 148:3-5:

Praise Him, sun and moon,
Praise Him all you shining stars!
Praise Him, you highest heavens,
And you waters above the heavens!
Let them praise the Name of the Lord!
For He commanded and they were created.

PARAGRAPH 19: Nineteenth Day of a Month

Read:

Mindful that they are bearers of peace which must be built up unceasingly, they should seek out ways of unity and fraternal harmony through dialogue, trusting in the presence of the divine seed in every one and in the transforming power of love and pardon. Messengers of perfect joy in every circumstance, they should strive to bring joy and hope to others. Since they are immersed in the resurrection of Christ, which gives true meaning to Sister Death, let them serenely tend toward the ultimate encounter with the Father.

Reflect:

All five of these ministries are truly ideal for Franciscans, be they promoting justice, work, family, creation or peace. But the latter, peace, is most intimately connected with us as bearers of peace. Do we have to be reminded how Francis strove to bring peace between Church and State, between Christians and Moslems, between Man and Animal, even between Life and Death? In every aspect of life, this was his prayer: *"May the Lord grant you peace!"* There is something truly transforming about peace. It's more than non-threatening: it actually frees the other to become open to listen and search for acceptable resolutions to conflict. It even frees me to face death as a loving Sister who cares for me and brings me to my final goal, union with God eternally.

Respond:

"Lord, make me an instrument of Your peace…." These words attributed to you, St. Francis, certainly capture your spirit. You teach us to be always bearers of peace with such greetings as *"The Lord grant you peace"* and *"Peace to this house"*. For you, as it should be for us, perfect joy would flourish, if we could only suffer adversity and still be at peace within ourselves. O Holy Spirit, lavish your fruits of peace, joy and hope upon us. But in order for me to share peace with others, I need to have that peace in my heart. Then, and only then, can I work alone and with others in the cause of peace, filled with confidence that God can ignite that spark of goodness in each person and situation. Only then can I face Sister Death as the final destination in my journey to God. *Pax et Bonum!*

Receive (Resolve):

Matthew 5:9 "Blessed are the peacemakers: for they shall be called children of God."

CHAPTER 3:
PARAGRAPHS 20 TO 26:

LIFE IN FRATERNITY:

PARAGRAPH 20: Twentieth Day of the Month

Read:

The Secular Franciscan Order is divided into fraternities of various levels – local, regional, national, and international. Each one has its own moral personality in the Church. These various fraternities are coordinated and united according to the norm of this rule and of the constitutions.

Reflect:

God has called us to salvation, not only as individuals, but also in community. While this is true for all the faithful, its significance is highlighted in how Secular Franciscans relate to each other - in Fraternity. But we start from the bottom up, rather than from the top down. Thus we begin as gatherings on the local level. From there we elect representatives from the local fraternities in a specific region to form a regional fraternity, and so on up the ladder to the national and international levels of fraternity. Having been active in a regional fraternity, make no mistake about it: these are real fraternal communities at each level. Every one not only has its canonical authority to exist, but each develops its own personality as its members seek to accomplish the experienced needs at each level.

Respond:

"O how good and pleasant it is for brothers and sisters to dwell together as one." In order to pray these words, the Psalmist had to know the great blessings of fraternity. For You teach us, Yahweh, that we are a people saved not only as individuals in isolation, but also in community. Thus it was (and is) that, Jesus, You still call sisters and brothers of the Secular Franciscan Order to gather in fraternity on several levels: starting from the bottom up with my own local fraternity, proceeding right through the regional, national and international fraternities. And each level should strive for true relationships in fraternity. Each of our levels are to reflect the aspirations and goals of the fraternities from which they flow. Therefore, may I be reminded to pray often: God, bless our fraternities on all levels with the gift of true community.

Receive (Resolve):

Acts 2:44-46 *"And all who believed were together and had all things in common day by day attending the temple together and breaking bread...."*

PARAGRAPH 21: Twenty First Day

Read:

On various levels, each fraternity is animated and guided by a council and minister (or president) who are elected by the professed according to the constitutions. Their service, which lasts for a definite period, is marked by a ready and willing spirit and is a duty of responsibility to each member and to the community. Within themselves the fraternities are structured in different ways according to the norm of the constitutions, according to the various needs of their members and their regions and under the guidance of their respective council.

Reflect:

As a citizen of a democratic nation, I have been proud of our history of free elections. Then

what am I to say about our Franciscan fraternities? We have had some 800 years experience electing local councils, whose representatives in turn elect councils at the higher level. Fortunately our councils have rather strict term limits, which minimizes the risk of stagnation in office. On the other hand, we're blessed with a flexibility which allows various structures to emerge which best meet our fraternal needs. Yes, I rightly rejoice in my nation's elections, but thank God more so for elections in our fraternities.

Respond:

Heavenly Father, I lift up in prayer all the servants who answer Your call to shepherd our fraternities at every level. Lord, continue to inspire competent brothers and sisters to minister to us. I stand in awe that for over eight hundred years our ministers and councilors have been elected by us professed members. Thank you for Your Divine Providence in this process because, human as we are, we couldn't have done it on our own, and still can't. Thank you also for the wisdom of Your Church down through these eight centuries, which has been called upon by us to assist us with its guidance.

Receive (Resolve):

Matthew 25:21 "Well done, good and faithful servant; you have been faithful over a little, I will set you over much; enter into the joy of your master."

PARAGRAPH 22: Twenty Second Day

Read:

The local fraternity is to be established canonically. It becomes the basic unit of the whole Order and a visible sign of the Church, the community of love. This should be the privileged place for developing a sense of Church and the Franciscan vocation and for enlivening the apostolic life of its members.

Reflect:

For all Secular Franciscans, it is at the local fraternity level where the rubber meets the road. For us it doesn't get more basic than this. We meet and relate at this level, seeking with the help of God to form real community. Male and female, young and old, every race and personality all struggling to become a sign of Church for all the world to see. Here in fraternity we have the unique opportunity to grow as faithful members of the Church and Order. Here, by our various individual and group ministries, we strive to take full part in the mission of the Church.

Respond:

Thank You, Lord, for my beloved local fraternity, the sisters and brothers who make it a community of love for me. I place each and every one of them before You. In a particular way, remember our precious sick and home bound, who worship with us from afar; unite their sufferings to Your own, for the benefit of the Church and Order at large. For it is here where I experience Church at my deepest level. Like a microcosm of the Church Universal, I encounter Clergy, Religious and Laity. My ongoing formation here equips me to venture forth with You in confidence, to carry out the ministries to which you have called me, where I go from Gospel to Life and Life to Gospel. I leave in Your loving care my former fraternities who welcomed, received, professed, and nourished me over the years.

Receive (Resolve):

Psalm 133:1 *"Behold, how good and pleasant it is when brethren dwell in unity."*

PARAGRAPH 23: Twenty Third Day

Read:

Requests for admission to the Secular Franciscan Order must be presented to the local fraternity, whose council decides upon the acceptance of new brothers and sisters. Admission into the Order is gradually attained through a time of initiation, a period of formation (*of at least 18 months in the U.S.A.*), and Profession of the rule. The entire community is engaged in this process of growth by its own manner of living. The age for profession and the distinctive Franciscan sign (i.e. Tau) are regulated by the statutes. Profession by nature is a permanent commitment. Members who find themselves in particular difficulties should discuss their problems with the council in fraternal dialogue. Withdrawal or permanent dismissal from the Order, if necessary, is an act of the fraternity council according to the norm of the constitutions.

Reflect:

Thank goodness there are competent professed who answer the call to serve on the council. The fulfillment of their duties are serious: the very life and growth of the fraternity depend upon them. It falls upon the council primarily, along with support of the members, that new candidates are accepted and led through the three stages of formation. But even after the newly professed accept the Tau as the outward sign of their Franciscanism, ongoing formation should continue for the rest of their lives. At times the council must make some gut wrenching decisions when members find themselves in difficult circumstances, including the possibility of withdrawal or dismissal. Lack of knowledge of our constitutions or their improper application by the council can lead to disastrous consequences. For example, one council did not realize that the period of formation in the United States was increased from 12 to 18 months. This misled the expectations of a candidate, resulting in alienation of the candidate and sponsors. Though service on the council is serious, at the same time it can be greatly rewarding.

Respond:

Lord, those who minister to us on the Council deserve Your special help and guidance. They have accepted Your call to serve at great personal sacrifice and effort. Upon them weighs heavily the burdens of discerning and permanently admitting new members. Although we are supposed to assist them in this gradual process of initiation, formation and profession, the bulk of responsibility falls on them. Particularly taxing are those problem situations which only they can decide with Your help, especially when withdrawal or dismissal are required. O Holy Spirit, be with them every step of the way. We call upon the graces promised them in their Baptism, Confirmation and Profession.

Receive (Resolve):

Luke 12:37 *"Blessed are those servants whom the master finds awake when he comes."*

PARAGRAPH 24: Twenty Fourth Day

Read:

To foster communion among members, the council should organize regular and frequent meetings of the community as well as meeting with other Franciscan groups, especially with youth groups. It should adopt appropriate means for growth in Franciscan and ecclesial life and encourage everyone to a life of fraternity. This communion continues with deceased brothers and sisters through prayer for them.
Reflect:

Community doesn't happen just by wishing it into existence. The regular gathering of the entire fraternity is *THE* single most important factor in building community. On regular and definitive intervals, we have to relate with each other in prayer, ongoing formation, working on common ministries and sharing fellowship. These interactions have their built in pushes and pulls, which must be resolved in a fraternal manner. Here we learn about each others needs and strengths. What's said here applies even more so to the council meetings, and is not restricted to one's own fraternity. We should foster regional gatherings as well as youth activities. Neither should our sick and deceased members be excluded from this fellowship. Community should involve regular visits to our sick as well as prayers for the repose of the souls of our dear departed.

Respond:

"And they devoted themselves to the Apostles' teaching and fellowship, to the breaking of bread and prayers." These words from Acts 2:42 beautifully sum up what our monthly fraternity gathering means to me. And, Lord, I'm grateful for the fellowship in the Parish Hall! Thank you for continuing to feed us when we pray from our ritual as well as extem-

poraneously from our hearts, confidently placing all our group and individual ministries in Your care, as well as our home bound. And keep inspiring our ongoing formation in the spirit of Clare and Francis. Lord, widen too our outreach beyond the confines of our local fraternity and parish. Deepen our relationship with our neighboring fraternities and our region at large. Never let us isolate ourselves from the young, the poor and even our deceased brothers and sisters. Yes, with Your guidance, carry our sense of community and sharing beyond the grave.

Receive:

I Corinthians 14:26 *"When you come together, each one has a hymn, a lesson….Let all things be done for edification."*

PARAGRAPH 25: Twenty Fifth Day

Read:

Regarding expenses necessary for the life of the fraternity and the needs of worship, of the apostolate and of charity, all the brothers and sisters should offer a contribution according to their means. Local fraternities as such are to contribute toward the expenses of the higher fraternity councils.

Reflect:

As good stewards of God's material blessings, we are expected to manage our personal and fraternity goods prudently. Just as we are expected to provide for our families and dependents adequately, so too should we do on behalf of our fraternal brethren. How many do we know who have unintentionally caused untold friction among the very ones they love, by not preparing an adequate will, even though their assets may be meager? That's pain that we can easily avoid. And isn't support one of the precepts of our Church? Why should things be so different in our spiritual family? We too want to provide for dignified worship, works of mercy, and the material needs of the fraternity. And don't forget the needs of our regional, national and international councils, so that they may continue to serve us. But as Secular Franciscans, we should never become so preoccupied with finances that we lose our perspective regarding our call to moderation and a spirit of detachment.

Respond:

"...this poor widow has contributed more than all of them: for they have given out of their abundance, but she out of her poverty...." Lord, we know that we must donate for the needs of the fraternity on all levels. Yes, we must provide for proper worship, charity, apostolates and other expenses. We know that our contributions to higher fraternities is a fraternity, not an individual obligation. But help us avoid preoccupation with material needs. In the spirit of Franciscan detachment, call to our minds the example of this poor widow; encourage each of us to contribute according to our means. Teach us also to order our personal and family finances aright and, like our Holy Father Francis, prepare an up-to-date Last Will and Testament.

Receive (Resolve):

II Corinthians 9:7 *"Each one must give as he has made up his mind, not reluctantly or under compulsion, for God loves a cheerful giver."*

PARAGRAPH 26: Twenty Sixth Day

Read:

As a concrete sign of communion and co-responsibility, the councils on various levels, in keeping with constitutions, shall ask for suitable and well prepared religious for spiritual assistance. They should make this request to the superiors of the four religious Franciscan Families, *(e.g. OFM, Capuchin, Conventual & TOR)* to whom the Secular Fraternity has been united for centuries. To promote fidelity to the charism as well as observance of the rule and to receive greater support in the life of the fraternity, the minister or president, with the consent of the council, should take care to ask for a regular pastoral visit by the competent religious superiors as well as for a fraternal visit from those of the higher fraternities, according to the norm of the constitutions (e.g. every 3 years.)

Reflect:

Oh, the great wisdom of our Franciscan family that recognizes that all three orders need each other! And although each order has its own special call and purpose, we share a relationship between us that is truly life giving. History has shown us how easy it is to feed in upon our individual groups and lose sight of our charism and common roles as Franciscans. We need to give and receive insightful feedback and we should be humble enough to ask for that assistance. Such requests raise problems of their own as we face a crisis in religious and priestly vocations. Despite that, we struggle to find ways to fulfill those needs of fraternal and pastoral visits.

Respond:

Jesus, we have committed ourselves to be faithful to the Franciscan spirit and rule, which Your Church has approved for us. We know that our spiritual growth is our own primary responsibility. But we can't do it alone: we need the example and assistance of the whole Franciscan Family. Please inspire and raise up more Spiritual Assistants from the Franciscans in the First, Second and Third Orders Religious to share their charism with us. We, on our part, promise to share ours with them, and to carry their Gospel message to the secular world. Help our fraternity minister, council and members prepare well for our pastoral and fraternal visits, so we that may benefit from the advice and counsel of our visitors. I praise you, Father, for calling us to be part of such a great spiritual family of mutual assistance; we don't have to go it alone!

Receive (Resolve):

Jeremiah 23:4 *"I will place shepherds over them who will tend them…."*

FOR ADDITIONAL DAYS OF THE MONTH, USE OTHER FRANCISCAN READINGS, e.g:

TWENTY-SEVENTH DAY OF THE MONTH:

BLESSING OF ST FRANCIS FROM HIS TESTAMENT:

Read:

"May whoever observes all this be filled in heaven with the blessing of the most high Father, and on earth with that of His beloved Son, together with the Holy Spirit, the Comforter."

Reflect:

What a comfort to know that St. Francis is up there in heaven, helping us by his intercession. He realizes better than we ourselves that we are still works in progress. Together we seculars have set out on a life-long journey to observe the Gospel of our Lord Jesus Christ, following in the footsteps of St. Francis. It's probably a good thing that we didn't fully realize the difficulties; then again neither did we foresee the joys. Once again we reaffirm our life-long commitment to this way of life.

Respond:

Holy Father Francis, thank you for this final blessing that you gave us before you made your *Transitus* to the other side. Please continue to bless us. Even in this blessing you still stress that Jesus revealed for us the awe inspiring relationship that the Blessed Trinity has within the Godhead. Once again we call to mind God's personal relationship with each of us as children of the Father, brothers and sisters of Christ, and receptive spouses continually inspired by the Spirit.

Receive (Resolve):

Matthew 28:19   *"Baptizing them in the Name of the Father, and of the Son and of the Holy Spirit."*

TWENTY-EIGHTH DAY OF A MONTH:

His Exhortation to us Brothers & Sisters of Penance:

Read:

"Oh, how happy and blessed are these men and women when they do these things and persevere in doing them, because "the Spirit of the Lord will rest upon them" and He will make "His home and dwelling among them" and they are the sons and daughters of the heavenly Father...."

Reflect:

The Lord turned the world's values upside down in His "Sermon on the Mount." And how many of us mortals struggle to appreciate them even today. Thankfully Francis was one of those that incorporated those Beatitudes into his new-found way of life. In his simple but profound way he showed us how to be truly happy: his Rule for us. Again he calls down God's blessing on us for putting his rule into practice.

Respond:

Thank You, Lord, for showing us where our real happiness and peace reside. Your Beatitudes confirm that we find joy in fulfilling Your will, yes, even perfect joy amid sorrow and persecution. For Your Spirit dwells within each of us, confirming our intimate relationship to the Father through His Son. Grant us perseverance to the end.

Receive (Resolve):

Matthew 4:12 – *"Rejoice and be glad….."*

TWENTY-NINTH DAY OF A MONTH:

His Exhortation (continued):

Read:

"…They are the spouses, brothers, and mothers of our Lord Jesus Christ. We are spouses, when by the Holy Spirit the faithful soul is united with our Lord Jesus Christ; we are brothers and sisters to Him when we fulfill "the will of the Father who is in heaven." We are mothers, when we carry Him in our heart and body through divine love and a pure and sincere conscience; we give birth to Him through a holy life which must give light to others by example."

Reflect:

I picture a vast crowd around Jesus as He is busy teaching and healing. Suddenly a messenger forces his way to Jesus, informing Him that His Mother and relatives are waiting to see Him. He responds quickly with a question: *"Who are My Mother and My brothers?"* Then He points to his disciples and says: *"Whoever does the will of My Father is Mother, brother and sister to Me."* Now some people might feel uncomfortable with His response, sensing a slight to His Mother... but not Francis. He sees a great mystery being revealed here: we are being called into a family relationship with the Blessed Trinity. By doing the Father's will, we become His daughters and sons, thus brothers to Jesus Himself. But Francis sees more: a spousal relationship with the Holy Spirit. As the Spirit overshadows Mary to conceive Jesus, in an analogous way, we lovingly receive Jesus in our hearts and give birth to Him by good example.

Respond:

Blessed Trinity, You continue to overwhelm me with the depth and intimacy of our relationships with You as children, siblings and spouses. But You compare us to the role of Your Mother. By the action of the Holy Spirit, we are to receive You, Jesus, lovingly in our hearts and then give birth to You by our good example. This is beyond our mere human comprehension! Praise God!

Receive (Resolve):

Luke 1:38 *And Mary said: "Behold, I am the handmaid of the Lord. Let it be done to me according to your word."*

THIRTIETH DAY OF A MONTH:

His Exhortation (continued):

Read:

"Oh, how glorious it is to have a great and holy Father in heaven! Oh, how glorious it is to have such a beautiful and admirable Spouse, the Holy Paraclete! Oh, how glorious it is to have such a Brother and such a Son, loved, beloved, humble, peaceful, sweet, lovable and desirable above all: Our Lord Jesus Christ, who gave up His life for His sheep...."

Reflect:

Surely you've noticed how I keep coming back to the way Francis constantly reminds us about our intimate relationship with each Person of the Holy Trinity. The Church must teach this, but somewhere along the way it never hit home for me. Certainly Jesus taught us that God is Our Father. Didn't He teach us the prayer by that name. And He also reinforced that we become His brothers by doing the will of His Father. But what about our relationship with the Holy Spirit? I can envision His overshadowing Mary at the Annunciation, mirroring His overshadowing the Ark of the Covenant. So why am I so uncomfortable with relating to the Holy Spirit as Spouse? The mystics down through the ages have actually experienced this spiritual union. Is it my masculine hang ups that impede my full acceptance of this relationship? Women seem much more comfortable than I. And yet He is the Beloved of my soul. And I really do want to enter fully into this mystery; somehow I suspect that it encompasses the whole mystery of the Church.

Respond:

Heavenly Father, make me more and more like Your Son, Jesus, by doing Your Will. He is my older Brother, the inspiration for my life. Stir up His Holy Spirit who dwells within me so that I may discern Your Will and receive His power to carry it out. Give me especially an openness to the mysterious way You desire to relate with me.

Receive (Resolve):

II Corinthians 13:14 *"The grace of the Lord Jesus Christ and the love of God and the fellowship of the Holy Spirit be with you all."*

THIRTY-FIRST DAY OF A MONTH:

Pope Paul VI Approved this Current 4th Rule in 800 Years:

Read:

"To use the words of our predecessor Pius IX, 'there never was anyone in whom there shone forth more vividly and who resembled more the image of Jesus Christ and the evangelical form of life than Francis.' We are happy that the "Franciscan Charism" today is still a force for the good of the Church and the human community....We approve and confirm with our apostolic authority and sanction the Rule

of the Secular Franciscan Order ....formerly called the Franciscan Third Order."

Reflect:

With these words, Pope Paul VI approved our present Rule, following in the footsteps of Innocent III, Nicholas IV and Leo XIII before him. Thus, this present version of our Holy Rule becomes only the fourth expression in about 800 years. What a credit to the spiritual genius of Francis who tied us and our rule to the judgment of the Supreme Pontiffs of the Universal Church! And down through these 800 years, countless Popes have provided invaluable guidance to us Brothers and Sisters of Penance, many of them to the point of becoming Secular Franciscans themselves. But we shouldn't be surprised because the Rule in all its forms brings up back to the timeless spirit of the Holy Gospel of Jesus, applied to the present needs of the Church today. Most likely there will arise a future expression, be it in 100 years or a thousand. If and when it happens, we can rest assured that it will keep us on the right track following the timeless Gospel of Jesus, in the footsteps of Francis.

Respond:

Thank You, Jesus, for inspiring Your Vicars to constantly confirm the charism of St. Francis and to consistently guide us, his spiritual family. Keep us faithful to the Chair of Peter which helps us fulfill our vocation in accord with the needs of the Church today.

Receive (Resolve):

Matthew 16:18   *"Thou art Peter...."*

APPENDIX

The *Lectio Divina* method of prayer may be applied to just about any meaningful spiritual work in addition to Scripture and the Third Order Rule. What we have prayed in the previous pages are merely samples of how to apply this method. However, many of these suggestions below, (as well as others), can prove particularly helpful for those of us called to follow Jesus in the footsteps of St. Francis. Other such suitable prospects for future prayer may be found from among the partial list of examples on the following pages:

Scriptural Sources:

Hebrew Bible:

    Moses and the Burning Bush
    Deliverance from Egypt
    Hear O Israel, your God is one
    The Ten Commandments
    The Call of Samuel
    The Book of Ruth
    Psalm 23: The Lord is My
        Shepherd
    Idols have mouths but speak not

Christian Bible:

    Healings as a result of Faith
    Healing of the father's epileptic son
    Woman who touched His tassel
    Healing the Centurion's servant
    One of the ten lepers gives thanks
    Teachings to help us live better:
    Love your neighbor as yourself
    Our Father
    Let the one without sin cast the first
        stone
    If you would be perfect, sell what
        you have and give to
        the poor and follow Me

Let the little children come unto Me
Take My yoke upon you and learn
    for I am meek and humble of
    heart
What would it profit a man if he
    gain the whole world yet
    suffers the loss of his soul
Where your treasure is
    there your heart will be
Store up your treasure where thief
    cannot steal nor moth
    consume
Wash the inside of the cup as well
    as the outside
Don't let your left hand know what
    your right hand is doing
Let not your heart be troubled
Sufficient for the day are the
    troubles thereof

Examples of Other Religious Sources:

Ejaculatory Prayers:
    My Lord and My God
    We Adore You, O Christ
    Jesus, I trust in You

Prayers:
    Lord, Make me an Instrument of
        your peace
    Soul of Christ, Sanctify Me

Hymns:

       You are All Beautiful, O Mary
Poems:
       Canticle of the Creatures
Creeds:
       Apostles' Creed
       Nicene Creed
Writings:
       Testament of St. Francis
       Exhortation to the Brothers and
           Sisters of Penance

N.B. In the following pages, by way of example, you can see how this method can be applied to two spiritual prayers.

SERENITY PRAYER
by
REINHOLD NIEBUHR

Read:

*God grant me
the <u>serenity</u> to accept the things I <u>cannot change</u>.
<u>Courage to change</u> the things I can
and <u>wisdom to know</u> the difference.*

*<u>Living one day at a time</u>,
enjoying one moment at a time.
Accepting <u>hardships as a pathway to peace</u>,
<u>taking as Jesus</u> did, this sinful <u>world as it is</u>,
not as I would have it.*

*Trusting that You will make all things right
if I <u>surrender to Your will</u>.
So that I may be <u>reasonably happy in this life</u>
and <u>supremely happy with You forever in the
next</u>.*

Amen!

Reflect:

Our brothers and sisters who are recovering from one addiction or another find great comfort and wisdom in this prayer. We too need that discernment to know what we can and cannot change in our lives. And we have to do it one day at a time. Too often we are so hung up on the past or worried about the future, we neglect to live in the present. The example of Jesus shows the way to peace. But, neither can I expect this life to be perfect; that's what heaven's for.

Respond:

Lord, Jesus, show me the way to be at peace with myself and my circumstances. So many of my problems stem from my refusal to accept the difficulties in my life. You've shown us that there can be redemptive value in suffering. Lord, I accept what you have in store for me.

Receive (Resolve): *Take one day at a time!*

FRANCISCAN PEACE PRAYER

Read:
Lord,
Make me an instrument of Your Peace
Where there is hatred,
Let me sow
love;
Where there is injury,
pardon;
Where there is doubt.
faith;
Where there is despair,
hope
Where there is darkness,
light;
Where there is sadness,
Joy.

O my Divine Master,
Grant that I may not so much seek
To be consoled as to console;
To be understood as to understand;
To be loved as to love;

For it is in giving that we receive;
It is in pardoning that we are pardoned;
It is in dying that we are born to eternal life.

Reflect:

The previous prayer leads me to a closer union with my Lord. This famous prayer teaches me what to do with that union: share it! Once we are in a deepening personal relationship with the Lord, He'll want to use us as His instruments to bring His peace to others. This gift of intimacy, His peace, He lavishes on us. We are to become His hands and heart to love, pardon, believe, enlighten and bring Joy. It's not what we get that counts, it's what we give.

Respond:

O God of Peace and Joy, You give Yourself to me without reservations. And I relish Your intimate presence within me. But You know how I am tempted to just rejoice in the strength of Your presence. Don't let me stay there, Lord! The intimate gifts You give are not for me alone. So use me, Jesus, to complete Your work among others. Saint Francis, speak to Jesus along with me.

Receive (Resolve):

It is no longer I who live, but Christ who lives in me.

COPY THIS FORMAT FOR *LECTIO DIVINA*

1.Read (and reread) slowly the passage you choose below , until you come to a word, phrase or section that strikes a chord in you and jot them down below:

_____
_____
_____
_____
_____
_____

2. Reflect on that section, word or phrase and consider what it's saying to you in your personal life. What does it mean to you where you're at (or want to be)? You can do this in the form or a letter to a fellow tertiary (or yourself), explaining what you got out of that paragraph:

Dear Fraternity Brother,

_____
_____
_____
_____
_____
_____
_____
_____
_____

3. Respond to God in prayer from your heart; just talk to God in your own words. It can be a letter to a Person of the Blessed Trinity, e.g.

Dear Jesus:

_____
_____
_____
_____
_____
_____
_____
_____
_____
_____
_____
_____

4. Receive (Resolve) gratefully whatever gifts the Lord may choose to give you. What specific resolve or resolution is He leading you to make now?

_____
_____
_____
_____

LIST OF PUBLICATIONS
BY
LUCAS J. AMATO, OFS

TYPE	TITLE	PULBISHER
CD	"Scriptural Meditations for the Divine Mercy Chaplet"	ACTA Publications
Book	"Scriptural Meditations for the Divine Mercy Chaplet, Franciscan Crown, 7 Sorrows, and Rosary"	ACTA Publications
Book	"Praying the WORD: Lectio Divina"	M & M Printing Co.
Book	"12 Steps and 12 Traditions: Applying the 11th Step".	Lulu.com
Book	"A Catholic Layman Prays Hebrew Scripture: Applying Lectio Divina in the Spirit of St. Benedict"	Lulu.com
Book	"Two Knights Pray the 12 & 12, Applying Knights of Columbus Principles, Lectio Divina, and A.A.'s 11th Step To Addictive & Enabling Behavior"	Lulu.com
Book	"Praying the Secular Franciscan Rule: Applying Lectio Divina as taught by St. Bonaventure, OFM"	Lulu.com

Made in the USA
Las Vegas, NV
21 January 2025